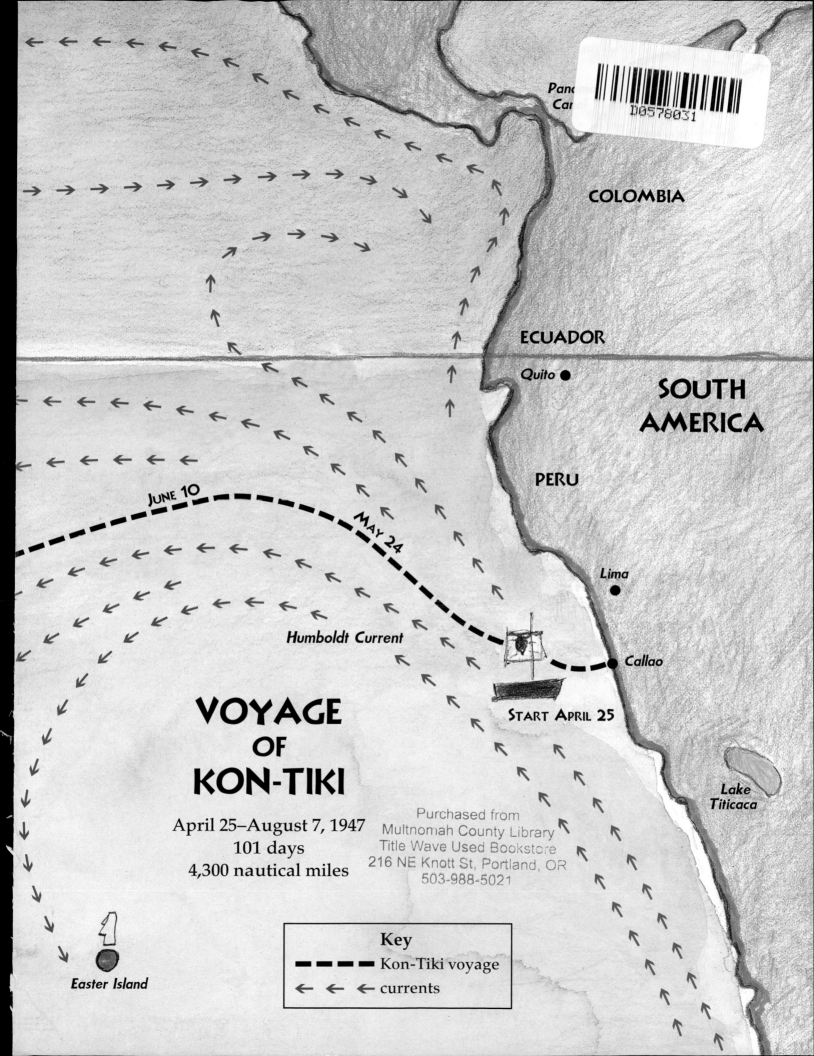

COLOMBIA

ECUADOR

Quito ●

SOUTH
AMERICA

PERU

Lima
●

Callao ●

JUNE 10

MAY 24

Humboldt Current

START APRIL 25

VOYAGE
OF
KON-TIKI

April 25–August 7, 1947
101 days
4,300 nautical miles

Lake
Titicaca

Easter Island

Key

━ ━ ━ Kon-Tiki voyage

↙ ↙ ↙ currents

"One day my theory was complete. I must go to America and put it forward."

—Thor Heyerdahl, Norwegian anthropologist, 1946

The
Impossible Voyage *of*
KON-TIKI

Deborah Kogan Ray

Charlesbridge

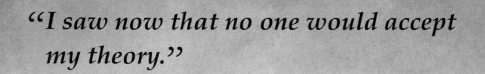

"I saw now that no one would accept my theory."

"Impossible!" declared the famous professor, shaking his head at Thor Heyerdahl.

It was not the first time the young Norwegian anthropologist had received such a response to his research project. He had arrived in New York City hopeful that scholars would be open to his theory that ancient Incans from South America had voyaged by raft to the islands of the South Pacific. But despite the evidence he presented, his idea was dismissed as speculation.

"Are you willing to try a forty-three-hundred-mile ocean trip on a primitive wooden raft to prove it can be done?" asked the professor, chuckling.

"It is my intention to prove that the journey is feasible."

Thor Heyerdahl's theory had been formed on the Polynesian island of Fatu Hiva, where he had lived for a year with the native people. The islanders had shown him stone carvings said to be of the mythic figure Tiki. According to legend, Tiki brought their ancestors from a land across the sea.

The carvings resembled statues made by ancient civilizations in South America. *Could the two cultures be related?* Thor wondered. Could there be a connection between the Polynesian Tiki and the Incan god Kon-Tiki Viracocha? Was it possible that ancient seafarers had crossed the Pacific Ocean to the South Sea Islands?

After ten years of his research being met with skepticism, Thor realized what he would have to do.

He decided to build a copy of an Incan balsa-log raft and reenact the voyage himself.

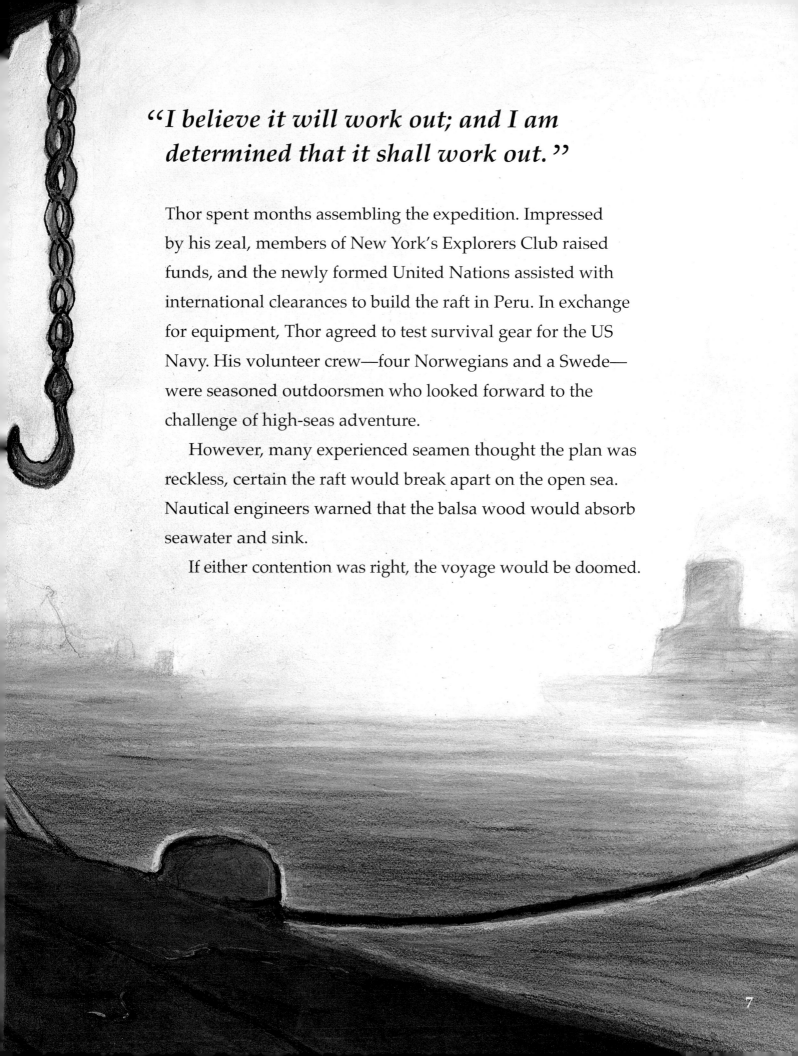

> *"I believe it will work out; and I am determined that it shall work out."*

Thor spent months assembling the expedition. Impressed by his zeal, members of New York's Explorers Club raised funds, and the newly formed United Nations assisted with international clearances to build the raft in Peru. In exchange for equipment, Thor agreed to test survival gear for the US Navy. His volunteer crew—four Norwegians and a Swede— were seasoned outdoorsmen who looked forward to the challenge of high-seas adventure.

However, many experienced seamen thought the plan was reckless, certain the raft would break apart on the open sea. Nautical engineers warned that the balsa wood would absorb seawater and sink.

If either contention was right, the voyage would be doomed.

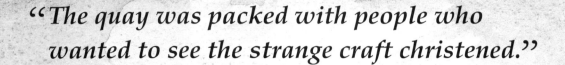

"The quay was packed with people who wanted to see the strange craft christened."

The raft was made of nine balsa logs lashed together with hemp rope. A bamboo cabin behind the single mast would provide the only shelter. The crew would bring minimal equipment: a sextant to determine position, shortwave radios to report their progress, and cameras to film the voyage.

Food supplies were limited because of weight considerations. Like ancient seafarers, the men would be dependent on the ocean's bounty.

On April 28, 1947, the *Kon-Tiki*—named after the Incan god—along with Thor Heyerdahl and his five-man crew, was towed out of Callao harbor, near Lima, Peru, and set adrift in the Humboldt Current.

> *"By late afternoon the trade wind was already blowing at full strength. It quickly stirred up the ocean into roaring seas."*

Contrary to all warnings, the *Kon-Tiki* proved to be seaworthy, and the current carried the raft farther and farther into the ocean.

They were now in the thrall of the powerful westward trade wind.

There was no turning back.

"After a week or so the sea grew calmer."

As the voyagers approached the Equator, a constant procession of pilot fish and dolphins joined them. At night, flying fish were attracted by light from the paraffin lamp and shot onto the deck and into the bamboo cabin—sometimes landing in bed with the men.

The only provisions aboard the raft were coconuts and dried sweet potatoes, but fresh food was always close at hand. The men baited lines with small squid and crabs to lure large tasty tuna and bonitos. They caught sharks by seizing their tail fins and hauling them on deck.

13

"We saw no sign either of a ship or drifting remains to show that there were other people in the world."

The *Kon-Tiki* existed as its own small world. Thor was constantly occupied with photographing and recording the voyage's daily activities in the logbook. His boyhood friend Erik Hesselberg was the only trained seaman aboard and was therefore in charge of navigation. Herman Watzinger, an engineer, was responsible for taking instrument readings of the weather and ocean. Knut Haugland and Torstein Raaby—both wartime radio operators—handled communications.

Bengt Danielsson oversaw food supplies, but cooking chores were divided equally, as was steering watch. Each man had two hours a day and two hours a night at the steering oar.

> "It often happened that the wind and sea remained unchanged for days on end. . . . The night watch could sit quietly in the cabin door and look at the stars."

Thor was on night watch just before midnight on July 2 when a ferocious wave suddenly swept up from the calm sea. He gave a warning shout as the *Kon-Tiki* was flung sideways. Rising out of the foam, another massive wave immediately followed. As the men struggled to hang on, a third wave struck.

As rapidly as the sea had risen up, it receded, and the three great waves raced on, leaving the men shaken and expectant. Were these rogue waves or a warning of things to come?

"*Two days later we had our first storm.*"

The storm began with a thick bank of black clouds moving fast from the south. Then gale-force winds erupted from different directions, churning the sea into a roaring vortex.

For a week the *Kon-Tiki* battled towering waves and torrential rains.

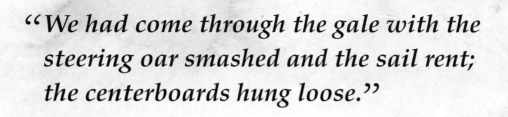

"We had come through the gale with the steering oar smashed and the sail rent; the centerboards hung loose."

Though the vessel was still afloat, the storm had taken a terrible toll on the *Kon-Tiki*. Without the centerboards to control direction, the raft was adrift, at the mercy of the wind and current.

The closest Polynesian islands lay more than three hundred miles ahead. To the northwest were Fatu Hiva and the Marquesas. To the southwest was the Tuamotu group. Between the two island chains was a great gap of open ocean.

Thor and the crew had no idea where the wind would carry them.

"Land. An island. We devoured it greedily with our eyes."

At sunrise on July 30, Thor awoke to Herman calling from the lookout on the masthead. Within moments Thor was up the ropes, shouting to wake the others. In the distance a short blue line of land was visible against the red morning sky.

According to Erik's sextant readings and navigation maps, the island that lay ahead was Puka-Puka, the farthest outpost of the Tuamotu group. As the *Kon-Tiki* drifted closer to land, Thor and the men watched with mounting excitement as treetops came into view.

But their joy was short-lived. A sudden wind rose up and pulled the raft, suddenly helpless, away.

"We knew that somewhere between us and the island was a dangerous submerged shoal."

Four days later the raft came so close to the atoll of Angatau that the islanders paddled out in canoes to welcome the *Kon-Tiki* seafarers and guide them past the shoal to safety.

But once again the strong wind and current swept the raft away, carrying it out to sea.

"We were drifting straight toward the ominous Takume and Raroia reefs."

There was no escape from imminent shipwreck.

In preparation, the crew packed documents into watertight bags and covered the bamboo cabin in canvas. Torstein continued to broadcast on the shortwave radio, hoping someone—somewhere—would pick up the distress call.

The men stood in readiness, each clinging fast to a rope, awaiting the inevitable crash.

"*I sank down on my knees and thrust my fingers deep down into the dry, warm sand.*"

On August 7, 1947, one hundred one days after leaving
Peru, the *Kon-Tiki* and its crew washed up on an uninhabited
island on the Raroia reef, in Polynesia. They had crossed
forty-three hundred nautical miles of the Pacific Ocean.
Thor Heyerdahl had proved that a primitive raft could
cross from South America to the South Sea Islands.

The impossible voyage was possible after all.

After the Impossible Voyage

On September 29, 1947, Thor Heyerdahl and his crew, along with the remains of the *Kon-Tiki*, arrived in the United States where they were greeted as heroes.

The "impossible" voyage of the *Kon-Tiki* had captured the imagination of people around the world. Heyerdahl and his crew had successfully crossed the Pacific Ocean—a journey of 4,300 nautical miles, equal to about 5,000 land miles (8,000 kilometers). Heyerdahl's 1950 book about the adventure, *Kon-Tiki: Across the Pacific by Raft*, became an international bestseller, was eventually translated into seventy languages, and is still in print. The movie he filmed during the voyage won the Academy Award for best documentary in 1951.

However, most scholars still dismissed Heyerdahl's migration theory. He had proven that a primitive raft could cross the Pacific Ocean from South America to Polynesia, but most scholars remained convinced, and still are today, that Polynesia was settled by an eastward migration from Asia.

Theories about how different parts of the world were populated have long been debated within academia. Though Heyerdahl's theory was controversial, he was not alone in his beliefs about early populations and migrations. He belonged to the group of anthropologists called diffusionists, who contend that ancient civilization spread across the world by land and sea.

Scientific advances, such as identifying heredity factors through DNA, have still not proven conclusively the origin of the earliest Polynesian settlers.

The Kon-Tiki (1947), *courtesy of the Kon-Tiki Museum, Oslo, Norway*

About Thor Heyerdahl (1914–2002)

Thor Heyerdahl (1951), courtesy of the Library of Congress

Thor Heyerdahl was born on October 6, 1914, in Larvik, a fishing town in southern Norway. Young Thor's mother was head of the local science museum and encouraged the boy to study nature. By the age of eight, he had become an enthusiastic collector of woodland animals and insects and dreamed about becoming an explorer.

At eighteen, Heyerdahl enrolled at the University of Oslo, where he majored in zoology. Before graduating, he lived for a year on the isolated Polynesian island of Fatu Hiva. While investigating the origins of the island's plant and animal life, Heyerdahl became intrigued by this question: From where and how did the islanders arrive on the Polynesian islands? These questions led to the voyage of the *Kon-Tiki* and began his remarkable career as an anthropological explorer.

After the *Kon-Tiki* expedition concluded, Heyerdahl also led an expedition to explore the "giant head" statues on Easter Island (1955–56), two expeditions to prove that ancient Egyptians had sailed vessels made from papyrus reed (*Ra* and *Ra II*; 1969–70), a journey aboard a reed vessel called *Tigris* to answer questions about civilizations in the Middle East (1977–78), and excavations of Peruvian ruins near Túcume (1998).

Heyerdahl raised major questions as part of his expeditions, not only about the past, but also about the future. He was one of the first people to warn others about the effects of pollution in the oceans, and through his writings, lectures, and work with the United Nations, he sought to awaken public awareness in order to find solutions to that ever-growing problem. Long before others recognized ecological damage to our planet, he advocated for a green world for current and future generations.

He kept a deeply held conviction all his life: that people should work with nature, not against it.

Heyerdahl lived out his last years on Tenerife, Canary Island, off the coast of Africa. He wrote an autobiography, *In the Footsteps of Adam* (2000), which is still in print in English. His last planned project was to return to the Pacific to do more research about the people of Polynesia.

He died of brain cancer on April 18, 2002, at the age of eighty-seven.

Further Information

The Kon-Tiki Museum in Oslo, Norway, has an excellent website that includes photographs and information about Thor Heyerdahl's life and expeditions. The raft *Kon-Tiki* is visited by thousands of people each year at the museum, where it is on display along with the papyrus boat *Ra II* and many other artifacts. **http://www.kon-tiki.no** (Click in the top right corner for English.)

Kon-Tiki, directed by Thor Heyerdahl (1951; Harrington Park, NJ: Janson Media, 2006), DVD.
   Heyderdahl's Academy Award–winning black-and-white movie was filmed during the 1947 voyage.

Kon-Tiki, directed by Joachim Rønning and Espen Sandberg. (2012; Beverly Hills, CA: Anchor Bay Entertainment, 2013), DVD.
   This 2012 Norwegian dramatization based on the *Kon-Tiki* voyage was filmed simultaneously in two versions: Norwegian and English.

Some films about Heyderdahl's other expeditions are available on YouTube. Search for *Ra*, *Tigris*, and *Easter Island* along with Thor Heyderdahl's name for clips.

Bibliography

Hesselberg, Erik. *Kon-Tiki and I*. Englewood Cliffs, NJ: Prentice Hall, 1970.
Heyerdahl, Thor. *Kon-Tiki: Across the Pacific by Raft*. Deluxe ed. Translated by F. H. Lyon. New York: Simon & Schuster, 1990.
Heyerdahl, Thor. *The Tigris Expedition: In Search of Our Beginnings*. New York: Doubleday, 1980.
———. *The Ra Expeditions*. New York: Doubleday, 1971.
———. *Aku Aku: The Secret of Easter Island*. New York: Rand McNally, 1958.
———. *Fatu-Hiva: Back to Nature*. New York: Doubleday, 1974.
———. *In the Footsteps of Adam: A Memoir*. Warwick, RI: Warwick Publishing, 2002.
Jacoby, Arnold. *Señor Kon-Tiki: A Biography of Thor Heyerdahl*. New York: Rand McNally, 1967.

Source Notes

title page: "One day . . .": Heyerdahl, *Kon-Tiki*, p. 19.
p. 2: "I saw now . . .": Heyerdahl, *Kon-Tiki*, p. 23.
p. 2: "Impossible!" and "Are you willing . . .": paraphrased from the account of Heyerdahl's 1946 meeting in New York with anthropologist Dr. Herbert Spinden, a past president of the Explorers Club and a curator and education director at the Brooklyn Museum, Jacoby, p. 217.
p. 4: "It is my intention . . .": Heyerdahl, as quoted in Jacoby, p. 218.
p. 7: "I believe . . .": Heyerdahl, as quoted in Jacoby, p. 227.
p. 8: "The quay . . .": Heyerdahl, *Kon-Tiki*, p. 68.
p. 11: "By late afternoon . . .": Heyerdahl, *Kon-Tiki*, p. 78.
p. 12: "After a week . . .": Heyerdahl, *Kon-Tiki*, p. 86.
p. 14: "We saw no sign . . .": Heyerdahl, *Kon-Tiki*, p. 96.
p. 16: "It often happened . . .": Heyerdahl, *Kon-Tiki*, p. 151.
p. 18: "Two days later . . .": Heyerdahl, *Kon-Tiki*, p. 154.
p. 21: "We had come . . .": Heyerdahl, *Kon-Tiki*, p. 162.
p. 22: "Land. An island. . . .": Heyerdahl, *Kon-Tiki*, p. 168.
p. 25: "We knew that somewhere . . .": Heyerdahl, *Kon-Tiki*, p.172.
p. 26: "We were drifting . . .": Heyerdahl, *Kon-Tiki*, p. 185.
p. 29: "I sank down . . .": Heyerdahl, *Kon-Tiki*, p. 198.

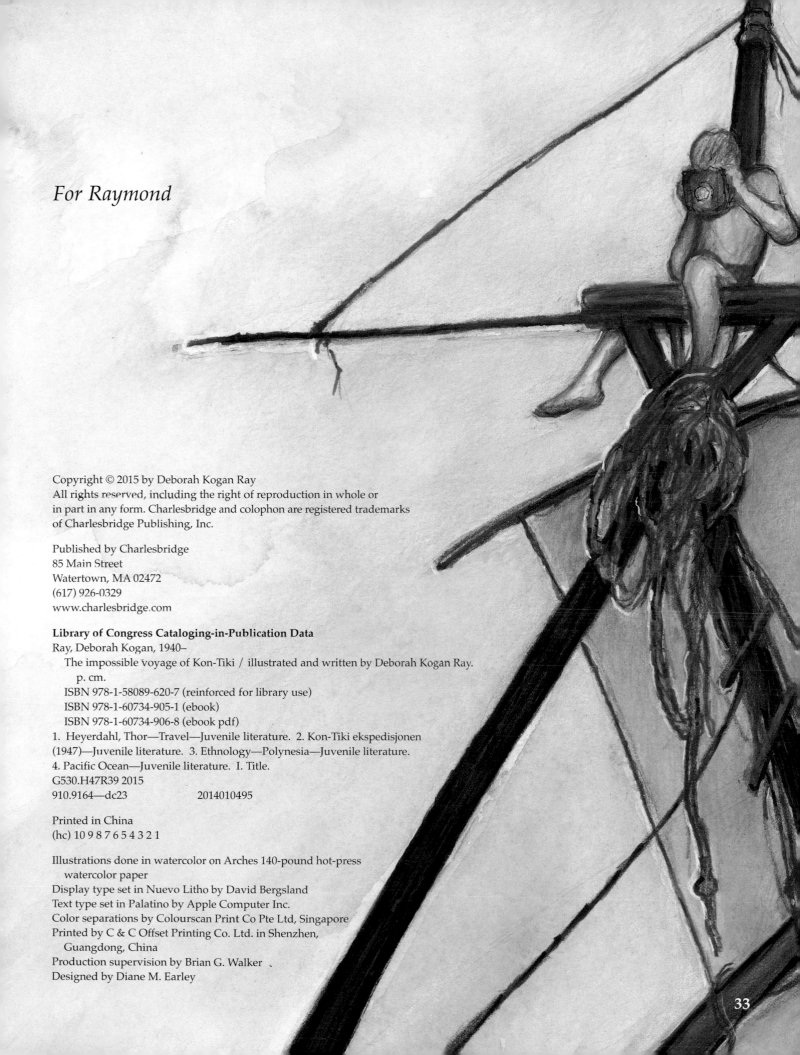

For Raymond

Published by Charlesbridge
85 Main Street
Watertown, MA 02472
(617) 926-0329
www.charlesbridge.com

Library of Congress Cataloging-in-Publication Data
Ray, Deborah Kogan, 1940–
   The impossible voyage of Kon-Tiki / illustrated and written by Deborah Kogan Ray.
      p. cm.
   ISBN 978-1-58089-620-7 (reinforced for library use)
   ISBN 978-1-60734-905-1 (ebook)
   ISBN 978-1-60734-906-8 (ebook pdf)
1. Heyerdahl, Thor—Travel—Juvenile literature. 2. Kon-Tiki ekspedisjonen
(1947)—Juvenile literature. 3. Ethnology—Polynesia—Juvenile literature.
4. Pacific Ocean—Juvenile literature. I. Title.
G530.H47R39 2015
910.9164—dc23   2014010495

Printed in China
(hc) 10 9 8 7 6 5 4 3 2 1

Illustrations done in watercolor on Arches 140-pound hot-press
   watercolor paper
Display type set in Nuevo Litho by David Bergsland
Text type set in Palatino by Apple Computer Inc.
Color separations by Colourscan Print Co Pte Ltd, Singapore
Printed by C & C Offset Printing Co. Ltd. in Shenzhen,
   Guangdong, China
Production supervision by Brian G. Walker
Designed by Diane M. Earley

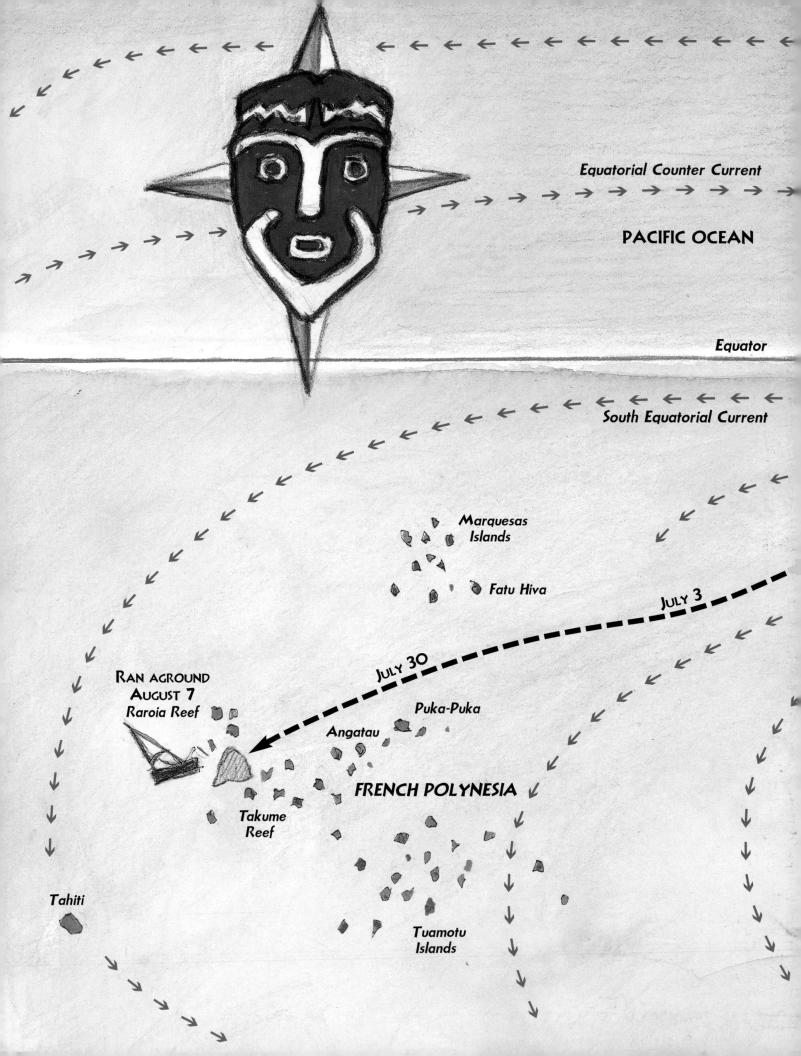